CONVICTION

The Pathway to Freedom

APRIL B. KNOLTON

WESTBOW
PRESS®
A DIVISION OF THOMAS NELSON
& ZONDERVAN

This book is a work of non-fiction. Unless otherwise noted, the author and the publisher make no explicit guarantees as to the accuracy of the information contained in this book and in some cases, names of people and places have been altered to protect their privacy.

WestBow Press books may be ordered through booksellers or by contacting:

WestBow Press
A Division of Thomas Nelson & Zondervan
1663 Liberty Drive
Bloomington, IN 47403
www.westbowpress.com
844-714-3454

Because of the dynamic nature of the Internet, any web addresses or links contained in this book may have changed since publication and may no longer be valid. The views expressed in this work are solely those of the author and do not necessarily reflect the views of the publisher, and the publisher hereby disclaims any responsibility for them.

Any people depicted in stock imagery provided by Getty Images are models, and such images are being used for illustrative purposes only. Certain stock imagery © Getty Images.

Author Contact: Email: aprilknolton@gmail.com

Author's Photo: Livin' For Media

Unless marked otherwise, all Scripture quotations are taken from the King James Version.

Scripture quotations marked NIV are taken from The Holy Bible, New International Version®, NIV® Copyright © 1973, 1978, 1984, 2011 by Biblica, Inc.® Used by permission. All rights reserved worldwide.

Scripture quotations marked AMP are taken from the Amplified® Bible, Copyright © 2015 by The Lockman Foundation. Used by permission.

Scripture quotations marked NLT are taken from the Holy Bible, New Living Translation, Copyright © 1996, 2004, 2015 by Tyndale House Foundation. Used by permission of Tyndale House Publishers, Inc., Carol Stream, Illinois 60188. All rights reserved.

ISBN: 978-1-6642-2453-7 (sc)
ISBN: 978-1-6642-2455-1 (hc)
ISBN: 978-1-6642-2454-4 (e)

Library of Congress Control Number: 2021903340

Print information available on the last page.

WestBow Press rev. date: 02/25/2021

This book is dedicated to Kayla Sani. Your birth is the very reason I had to stand on the principle of love. You are the reason I fight so hard in prayer! I always want you to physically feel and see an example of a mother's love toward her daughter. I want you to feel like you can always call your mom and be secure, convinced that I will be ready to receive you. All generational deficits of motherly love were broken when God gave me you!

Contents

Acknowledgments

I reverence God for this opportunity to put into words what's in my heart.

Thank you to my lovely parents for giving me life and loving me with all that's within you. I love you. Without you, there'd be no me. Mom, thank you for making so many sacrifices as I was growing up! Love you, Mom and Dad!

To my Bonus Dad, sisters, brother, and nephew: I love you all so much and thank you for being beautiful and loving!

To my dearest family, friends, and sisters, Shanetta, Keisha, Kim J., Cheryl, Delean, Kanisha, Carmita, LaToddra, Tiffany J., Makol, Meaghan, Brenda, and Bianca. Thank you for all the help! I love you all so much, and I couldn't have imagined missing any part of this journey I experienced without any of you! Our adventures may not consist of day in and day out interactions, but at some point you all encouraged me when I couldn't encourage myself! Thank you!

To evangelist Mary "Toni" Flowers and every apostle, bishop, pastor, first lady, prophet, prophetess, elder, minister, deacon, evangelist, missionary, mother, and teacher who has blessed me in some way or another. Thank you!

I am thankful for every life situation that I've incurred and conquered. I never felt it then, but those opportunities were preparing me for something greater: being made whole! Thank you all, and I love you!

Prologue

There was a certain woman caught in the act of adultery. She was apprehended by her accusers, who were in fact correct regarding their allegations of her. She was caught amid a sinful offence, and her sentence was to be stoned according to the law of that time. Before rendering a verdict, the people sought the council of Jesus, hoping to lure Him into a scandal or act of lawbreaking as well. Instead of speaking against the law that Moses commanded regarding adultery, within the midst of the people, Jesus stooped down and began to write on the ground, as if to ignore them. The men waited for Jesus to release a response to their questioning and had already gathered stones, prepared to cast them at the adulterous woman.

Jesus's statement cut into the core of their consciousness and soul. He said in John 8:7b, "He that is without sin among you, let him first cast a stone at her." After that, Jesus went back to writing on the ground. The mob was still standing there to cast a stone, but they couldn't do it! Verse 9a goes on to say, "And they which heard it being convicted by their own conscious, went out one by one, beginning at the eldest, even unto the last."

There was a power within the conscious of each of them so strong that it crippled them from legally putting the woman to death by stoning. It was at this very point in scripture that I began my transition to understand conviction from the perspective of freedom. Have you ever stopped to think about what that really means? Only a person who is sin-free of everything in the world, from birth to adulthood, could cast a stone! But how do we as worldly humans escape sin? All humanity is sinful at birth, even from the moment of conception (see Psalm 51:5). The accusers were not sin-free and were convicted by their own conscious according to the Bible. I wondered, What is so powerful about conviction?

The authority of the conviction process caused a guilty woman to escape from death without speaking a word of defense for herself! I was in amazement at how something could be so powerfully influential in the thought patterns of humanity. I was intrigued by this passage of scripture and desired to learn more. I immediately began researching and looking for books, articles, and writings on conviction but wasn't very successful. I acquired many resources with law-bearing attributes or literature containing scandals, deception, or murder, but that wasn't what I was looking for.

I aggressively searched more only to find court proceedings and information on convictions resulting in imprisonment or other legal matters. I asked, Why are we overlooking the process, focus, and reality of conviction in our lives? I believed within my heart that conviction played a substantial part in the human conscience. I continued seeking until I received greater revelation from God. After much toiling on my end, God pressed upon my heart to investigate my personal life for the answers.

I obeyed God, and afterward my awareness of my personal convictions heightened. I began to process the thought that convictions are principles that we stand on even in the face of death. Convictions are harbored in our conscious, good or bad. Having convictions are essential to our life and our character. They are principles that lead and guide every decision that we make.

Let's revisit this biblical example. In the lowest point of a shamefaced moment, facing the daunting truth of a guilty verdict, the power of conviction changed a decision from death to life, from conviction and sentencing to conviction and freedom to live on. No case was fought and no defense was made, only the thought within oneself that had the ability to provoke a thought so riveting that everyone holding a stone to kill the adulteress woman was compelled to drop it and walk away. Those men were convicted, convinced, and completely certain that they had sinned at some point in their personal lives. Conviction gives the ability to cause life and set

Chapter 1

CONVICTION VERSUS CONVICTION

What is conviction? Conviction, according to Merriam-Webster, is

> 1: the act or process of finding a person guilty of a crime especially in a court of law

> 2a: a strong persuasion or belief; b: the state of being convinced

> 3a: the act of convincing a person of error or of compelling the admission of a truth; b: the state of being convinced of error or compelled to admit the truth.

Nelson's New Illustrated Bible Dictionary says it's "the process of being condemned by one's own conscious as a sinner because of God's demand."

Why conviction? Conviction was birthed out of the curiosity of the word itself. While reading a familiar passage of scripture, the word *conviction* leaped out like a frog springing from one lily pad to another. I immediately envisioned a jail cell closing before me with a loud clanking sound, symbolic of the bars closing in my face. I went on to further process it and determined that conviction was a horrible place to be if sentenced, whether one was guilty or not. I was curious to take a second look and gain a deeper understanding of this life-altering word.

Conviction has the same spelling and sound, but opposing meanings. This lured me deeper to learn how this could potentially and significantly affect someone's life. Then I had a defining moment while researching. I discovered the intent of the second meaning of conviction! I contemplated whether I truly believed a word that carries negativity and captivity could also produce fruit of great change without being bound and offer freedom.

Conviction has another meaning beyond judgment, verdicts, and sentencing in a court of law. It also holds a spiritual meaning that personifies a firm position, belief, or principle, as well as the quality of presenting a convincing or compelling stance of one's beliefs. In its second meaning, it's one that allows God to move within our conscious to invoke change and establish our belief systems and principles until death. I found there are three major workings of conviction: law, beliefs, and Holy Spirit. I also realized we have countless personal convictions. Our convictions define the culture in which we believe and carry out in our lives and daily routines.

Ultimately, there are three major workings of conviction: conviction of the law (James 2:12), beliefs (Acts 2:37), and the Holy Spirit (John 16:8). However, there are countless personal convictions that we may uphold in our daily lives and routines. These are principles that people have chosen individually that shape their actions, thought patterns, and decisions. Convictions are principles we're convinced of through experiences, testimonies, and truths exposed within our lives. Ultimately, wherever there is a stance without wavering or change, no matter the outcome or influence of other people or situations, that's an area of conviction.

CONVICTION OF THE LAW

> Speak and act as those who are going to be judged by the law that gives freedom. (James 2:12 NIV)

When the law is broken, there are consequences that may follow. What happens after the guilty verdict is in and a person becomes a convicted criminal in a court of law? In most cases, sentencing immediately follows. Whether it's a monetary loss or quality time with loved ones, a guilty sentence is life-changing. After a guilty sentence is entered, the convict's name and identity is tarnished, potentially for the remainder of his or her life.

The primary reason this happens is because a guilty sentence is a condemning occurrence. Worldly conviction brings forth condemnation, rejection, guilt, shame, fear, and many other faults one might wrestle against. What does it mean to condemn? A couple meanings from Merriam-Webster is "to declare to be reprehensible, wrong, or evil usually after weighing evidence and without reservation; to pronounce guilty." In other words, wherever there is worldly conviction, you'll find condemnation.

Biblically speaking, in Jesus, there is no condemnation. Romans 8:1 (AMP) says, "Therefore there is now no condemnation [no guilty verdict, no punishment] for those who are in Christ Jesus [who believe in Him as personal Lord and Savior]." After a guilty verdict is rendered in a court case, people are sentenced (condemned) according to the laws of the world. But when you are convicted by God, there is awareness for the need to change; it releases freedom and gives salvation.

> For [godly] sorrow that is in accord with the will
> of God produces a repentance without regret,

leading to salvation; but worldly sorrow [the hopeless sorrow of those who do not believe] produces death. (2 Corinthians 7:10 AMP)

The adversary (Satan) wants you to believe conviction is equivalent to condemnation so that you willingly accept shame, guilt, and torment. For this reason, it's imperative to understand the premise of conviction being a pathway into Christ's freedom!

This is what James meant when he was advising the people to resist becoming guilty of the laws of the land. He encouraged them to be convicted by the law of liberty, which is in Christ. Conviction is a way out. Reclaim your life by understanding that convictions of weights and sins lead to freedom. Remember: it's the same word, but there are different meanings! In retrospect, the ideal of someone being excited about a conviction seems daunting. However, conviction is bigger than alienation in a prison cell. It's the beginning process of one's conscious awareness, along with an assured confidence in that belief system.

Having convictions causes one to mentally address strengths or faults, both naturally and spiritually. Naturally, having laws in place means keeping order. At times the justice that laws should bring is not upheld or may discriminate toward individuals or groups of people, but it is important to have recourse for some level of accountability. In many instances, it's easily recognizable that the law is being broken. For example, if you're speeding, you know based on the vehicle's speedometer and the posted speed limit signs that you're going too fast. Another example is in most cultures, murder is wrong or sinful.

Awareness of God moving upon us to convict, may not be known or received as easily. We have a choice to believe, to change, or to remain the same. God's conviction can feel uncomfortable to our norm but opens our hearts to a deeper and greater personal understanding. Use discernment without bias of God's righteous judgments, and consider cooperating, trusting, and having faith in what He is showing you.

Ask yourself, "Do I break or uphold the law?"

CONVICTION OF BELIEFS

> Now when they heard this, they were pricked in their heart, and said unto Peter and to the rest of the apostles, Men and brethren, what shall we do? (Acts 2:37)

What do you believe? That is the question to answer. *Believe* is an action word, a verb. There must be a transition from one course of thought to another. Merriam-Webster defines *believe* as "to consider to be true or honest; to accept the word or evidence; to hold as an opinion; to accept something as true; to have a firm or wholehearted religious conviction or persuasion: to regard the existence of God as a fact; to have a firm conviction as to the goodness, efficacy, or ability of something."

My personal interpretation of my beliefs in God is to make the choice to shift from worldly perspectives to accept biblical and godly principles. There are usually skeptics surrounding any belief system. You must have a solid conviction and position to avoid structural damage to your foundation of beliefs due to skepticism.

For many years, I heard people talking about God. I'd think, *Well, where is God?* The more I aged and digested the tragedies in my life, the more I questioned whether God was real. I didn't grow up in a religious family and didn't regularly attend church. Children were sent to church in a church van whenever the option was available, especially on Easter! I don't remember any messages preached or scriptures. I remember a lady falling straight back and hitting her head on a water fountain. I didn't know going to church was a God thing! There was no consistency in when or where we went; it was whichever church van picked us up the quickest.

I chose to start with my background so you would understand the fallacies I had in my personal beliefs. My believing did not come from being taught as a child; it came from my personal encounters with God. I didn't write this book because of my lineage within the ranks of church polity.

I wrote this book because of my relationship and obedience to the true and living God, Jesus Christ, in whom I believe. Throw out all assumptions that my childhood culture is why I believe God's Word. I heard His Word and accepted God's Word by faith. There was no coercing!

Acts 2 is a notable example of adding believers to the kingdom of God. Jesus had ascended back into heaven, and His disciples and followers were waiting in the upper room for His promise: the Holy Spirit. After the Holy Spirit fully came to earth, there was a sound from heaven—the appearance of tongues resembling fire that separated and settled on each person in the upper room. They were all filled with the Holy Spirit and then spoke in different languages. People from every nation under heaven were there at the time watching.

The spectators were astonished and amazed with the experience they had witnessed firsthand. They thought the followers of Christ were drunk! They were curious to unfold how these men, who were unlearned, had the ability to speak in their language so suddenly. They couldn't process what had just taken place; they carelessly looked at the outward appearance of the men and concluded that they were drunken. Peter stepped up and spoke with a confident voice and presented salvation through the blood of Jesus Christ to the spectators.

With their personal observations and what they'd heard about Jesus, they were convicted in their conscious and received Jesus immediately. Conviction began when the unexplained happened, the people were convinced of God's Word and believed the evidence they witnessed and experienced. Conviction is personal; you may share similar or the same convictions as another person, but the conviction process works on every person individually and takes effect at different times. In Acts 2, the people were convicted due to the evidence seen of the Holy Spirit and the word of God.

Ask yourself, How did I come to the point of believing?

CONVICTION OF THE HOLY SPIRIT

> And He, when He comes, will convict the
> world about [the guilt of] sin [and the need for
> a Savior], and about righteousness, and about
> judgment. (John 16:8 AMP)

The Holy Spirit is essential to living a righteous life! He is the third member of the Trinity. He convicts unbelievers of their sin, leads them to confessing Jesus Christ as Lord, and baptizes them into the body of Christ from the moment of repentance. The Holy Spirit speaks to the conscious of an individual encouraging positive choices. There is no reason to fear Him!

There is, however, a misconception that He only makes one speak in an unknown tongue or run around screaming. He serves in various daily roles so that a believer can experience the fullness of God. You don't "catch" the Holy Ghost despite widespread belief; He is a gift given freely from God to those who receives Him. Some of the workings of the Holy Spirit in the lives of believers today are that He lives in us, leads, guides, teaches, and does so many other things.

There's no benefit in rejecting the Holy Spirit because He equips the believer for holy living. God's Word is not tainted, Jesus is not tainted, and the Holy Spirit is not tainted. Sometimes the person or people representing can be tainted. I often say, "If sin is the disease and Jesus is the antidote, then why would you, as the believer, walk around as the infection? Infected folks infect others!" It's important to openly walk in the fruit of the Spirit as outlined in Galatians 5:22, "Love, joy, peace, longsuffering, gentleness, goodness, faith, meekness, temperance: against such there is no law." I pray that your first thought of the word *conviction* will no longer rest in bondage alone, but the freedom to walk out God's desired pathway for your life!

He wants us to live clean and holy lives, putting down every obstacle, sin, or distraction. But in order to know the difference, there must be a root of having strong convictions. My convictions are not yours, and vice versa, but understand that at some point, accountability must be given for every decision made. Allow God to speak to your heart and mind daily! When you feel a tugging in your heart, open it up to what the Holy Spirit wants to do in your life.

Prayerfully, you're imagining how these convictions may work in your life. Condemnation could result from breaking the law and immoral choices. If found guilty, a person is apprehended, convicted, and sentenced! One's life then changes in a negative and condemning way. This can also impact every person associated with the person due to their connection with that sentenced individual.

Sometimes our moral convictions may trouble our hearts when we attempt to do wrong. This is true for convictions that lead to changes spiritually as well. One goes from unbeliever to believer; from sinner to saint. Being convicted and exhibiting the fruit of having godly sorrow is evident in one that has chosen the pathway of repentance, which then provides the path to conversion and daily change to grow as a new convert of Jesus Christ. A conviction of belief is the foundational basis for how a person chooses to live. Whether that conviction is in the existence of God and His doctrine written in the Holy Bible or the belief of other gods or systems, it's what one believes no matter the consequences.

Conviction of the Holy Spirit is complete acceptance of the Trinity, God the Father, God the Son, and God the Holy Spirit. The Holy Spirit is the gift that Jesus promised to aid believers in the earth (John 14:26; John 15:26; John 16:7). Note that it is possible to have a conviction of belief but not of the Holy Spirit. Everyone has the freedom and a right to uphold a belief. Even in Christendom, there are some who do not believe in the Trinity, which could dismiss a conviction of the Holy Spirit. Are you ready to stand on your elections no matter what?

Ask yourself, "How much will my life be affected if I yield to God's conviction process? How many people can I personally encourage and uplift through my convictions? What testimonials and evidence do I have to share that will promote a positive outlook on being convicted?"

Chapter 2

CONVICTIONS VERSUS PREFERENCES

Let's begin by defining *preference* as we've previously defined *conviction*. Merriam-Webster's says that *preference* is "the act of preferring: the state of being preferred; the power or opportunity of choosing; one that is preferred; the act, fact or principle of giving advantages to some over others; priority in the right to demand and receive satisfaction of an obligation." Basically, it's the choices or decisions we make that are driven by our personal satisfaction.

Preferences are points of personal interest that may change periodically and could feel like a conviction until the need to satisfy something occurs. For example, you've hated pink your entire life, but then a new shade of pink is introduced to the world, and now you decide you must try it. The preference is the decision to try the new shade of pink, although you previously hated pink. Another is if you've always steered clear of legumes because you absolutely hate them. But one day there's no food left to eat except legumes, so you eat them because you don't want to starve. Our preferences may in fact change due to adapting to situations we face.

Those were both examples of being against something until there was a demand and need to receive satisfaction. That is the distinguished difference between convictions and preferences: one never changes, and the other changes frequently. Oftentimes we confess convictions of diverse types, but they are in fact only preferences.

Allow me to give a condensed summary of Acts 6–7, where we find a man named Stephen, the first Christian martyr. The Bible says the choice of Stephen pleased the people. Stephen held qualities and characteristics that delighted the congregants so much so that the suggestion of Stephen in a leadership role pleased them. Stephen was described as a man of faith in Jesus filled with the Holy Spirit. Stephen was selected to serve the people food daily.

An attitude of grace and blessings were upon him as he submitted himself as a servant leader doing great wonders and miracles. Stephen was using his gifts and talents given by God to serve and be a blessing to the people. Unfortunately, he was secretly being plotted against. The very people he was serving were conspiring for his arrest, conviction, and sentencing. Although Stephen was serving everyone, everyone was not happy about his teachings and demonstrations of the power of God.

Stephen was apprehended and brought before the council, which had already reached a verdict. During the questioning of Stephen before the council, they saw his face light up like that of an angel. In the face of the biased, unjust, cruel, and evil treatment executed upon Stephen, he continued to stand on his conviction of Christ. He remained committed to his conviction of God's Word. He remained submissive in his conviction of the Holy Spirit. He remained convicted to the pathway of God, unmovable, and unwavering! Although facing death, Stephen saw Jesus standing at the right hand of God, and his convictions continued as he prayed unto the Lord Jesus with a loud cry until he died.

A true conviction will go with you to the grave. I can truthfully say I've called things convictions when they were merely preferences. Many preferences had come and gone, but my convictions were always there no matter where I was in my life. Since understanding the differences between the two, I began to condemn myself in areas where I realized I should have honored or had convictions but didn't. Some of the choices I made weren't so good, and I felt horrible when I looked back over my life. Momentarily I missed the key point about conviction: it brings forth freedom, not condemnation!

The most assuring aspect of conviction is personal freedom from bondage or imprisonment of your consciousness. The consciousness is where you find you! It's the place where everything is happening, your thoughts, and the central location of your inner workings. Every human being has a consciousness, which is where conviction takes place. We are all made up of body, spirit, and soul. Our consciousness is centered in the heart of our souls, which is the essence of who we are. Our perceptions and will are birthed out of our consciousness. Feelings and notions function through our consciousness. Which are then filtered into our life's decisions and preferences.

It's very important to know the difference between your preferences and convictions. Having solid knowledge and distinction of the two makes a greater and more substantial influence on your decisions. Throughout this manuscript, you'll find Bible scriptures, stories, and my personal testimonies. Keep in mind that convictions are always a personal journey and not one that everyone will understand, relate to, or even care about. Whether the awareness brought by conviction warrants a response to repent, change, or make healthier choices, it is the pathway to being set free! Everyone is equipped with the power to choose a pathway. Make your choice today!

Chapter 3

CONVICTION VERSUS CONDEMNATION

There is a difference between having a conviction and feeling condemned. The scriptures declare in Roman 8:1 (NIV), "Therefore, there is now no condemnation for those who are in Christ Jesus" It is also written in John 3:17–18, "For God sent not his son into the world to condemn the world; but that the world through him might be saved. He that believeth on him is not condemned: but he that believeth not is condemned already, because he hath not believed in the name of the only begotten Son of God." God loved us so much that He sent His Son, Jesus, as our pardoning leverage from sin—if we repent. Therefore, abolish the belief that God is always looking for you to pay Him back! Stop believing that

He is a tit-for-tat God! Stop thinking that He sits high and looks low just to pick on you!

God is not a bully, nor is He petty. There is no condemnation in Christ Jesus! Every decision we make has a consequence, whether it's good or bad. Personally speaking, I would associate bad happenings with me disobeying God's Word all the time. For example, if I got a hang nail, the first thing I would think is, "I shouldn't have taken that pen from work." What? I know stealing is wrong, but God is not going to give me a hangnail because I took a pen that wasn't mine!

In retrospect, I was never trying to steal the pen. Maybe I was writing something as I was preparing to leave for the day. Naturally, on the business side of things, employees may not get raises, perks may be taken away, and jobs may get cut. This is the consequence of inadvertently increasing the company's spending on supplies due to employee theft. It is not God trying to take you out! I had a very hard time considering the actuality that I am not condemned. A portion of the problem was that I was condemning others.

Regularly, I sought judgment for people who hurt me or anyone close to me. I was condemning others but expecting mercy if I or my people were the offender. With that principle in which I operated under, I assumed God had to be the same way. The Scripture clearly speaks against condemnation and does not testify of this behavior as being any traits or characteristics of God the Father, God the Son, and God the

Holy Spirit (the Trinity). I was so consumed with the world's judicial aspect of conviction that I assumed God might secretly be the same way. I admit that I was wrong, of course!

My concept was wrong, my perception was wrong, and quite frankly I was being too carnal minded! I transposed condemning for chastening. Biblically, chastening and conviction describe terms of God working in our lives for our repentance. Jesus said in Revelation 3:19, "As many as I love, I rebuke and chasten: be zealous therefore and repent." Just as our natural parents want the best for us, God wants the best for us in this life and eternally. Just as our natural parents look to build us up, God looks to build us up. If we can endure correction and chastisement, we'll witness maturity operating in difficult times of our lives. Chastisement may feel like a whipping or punishment, but it works out in our favor in the end, plus it's not condemnation!

Chastisement doesn't leave you locked up and cast away. It will not blemish your identity and cause rejection because you've been found guilty. I'm not a fan of being chastised because I don't like how it feels; it's hard to go through. But who takes joy in being corrected? When I didn't like something, I associated it with being punished or condemned. God convicted me through His Word of this mindset; I was stuck in a vortex of unhealthy thinking.

God loves me so much that He reminded me through His Word, "Now no chastening for the present seemeth to be joyous, but grievous: nevertheless afterward it yieldeth the peaceable fruit of righteousness unto them which are exercised thereby (Hebrews 12:11)." Also in Proverbs 3:11, "My son, despise not the chastening of the LORD; neither be weary of his correction:" Understand that God's chastisement has intentional purpose attached to it.

Whether it's to rebuke, educate, instruct, or correct, it helps us become disciplined in the doctrine that we believe. We know that God does it because He loves us, just as natural parents do what is necessary to get us to make positive choices. With God, when I make poor choices, I'm still not condemned! Of course, I press daily not to condemn myself or others because that doesn't edify anyone. As believers, we must be aware of the difference between being forgiven of sin and being condemned by sin.

These are two different concepts. The ways of God are always leading us to repentance. He wants all to come to repentance, but it must be a personal decision. That's why He doesn't condemn us, because He is still trying to reach our hearts. His judgment will come, but if there is still time, receive Him before the only option you have is death. Romans 6:23 says, "For the wages of sin is death; but the gift of God is eternal life through Jesus Christ our Lord." I want to be clear that when we reject Christ, we're rejecting the antidote to sin and have chosen to be condemned.

The world can submit a judgment against you, put you on

trial by jury, and impose a sentence to the judge—but God doesn't operate like that! He gives us an opportunity through the process of conviction to see a mistake and correct it before it becomes an error. Operating in the spirit of error can cause nations to fall and people's lives to be ruined. Be mindful of the freedom that conviction brings; it makes evident that condemnation is not God's choice for our lives.

I can't tell you how to let yourself off the hook, but what I can tell you is to try. Pursue conviction of freedom that enables you not to condemn yourself. The first thing you should do is identify the cycle or the systemic root of your thoughts of condemnation. Stand in the truth in order to combat the lies of the enemy and everything that exalts itself above the knowledge of Christ! God loves you, He created the world for you, He made provisions for you, and He sent His son for you!

It gives me hope that although I may step outside the borders, God is not going to exile me but rather will guide me back to the right pathway through correction and chastisement. That is what a loving father would do. Therefore, I know I am not condemned—I'm loved!

Let go of all thoughts that you are bound by your past or decisions you've made that were not edifying to yourself or others. You are not condemned, so let yourself off the hook and walk in liberty!

Chapter 4

SELF-LOATHING

Let's move on to personal convictions, which are immeasurable because they're individual elections. My desire is to stir readiness so that you're encouraged to examine your personal convictions and feel empowered to stand on them. We've made it to the first chapter holding one of my most triumphant personal convictions. By far this was the most difficult area of accepting and walking in conviction. To stand on self-love was such a scary concept for me. I'd always ask the daunting question, How could I truly love another if I don't love myself? You read that right! I had a challenging time loving myself for years.

God allowed me to find myself in His Word. It was very interesting to see things as God did. I did so much self-persecution and negative speaking over my life that I had no idea that I was speaking directly against God. At that time, I never considered that who I was reflected the image of God. I refused to believe that genuine compliments were nothing more than hidden insults and character assaults. I was convinced that everyone saw me just as I had viewed myself: negatively!

I believed that everyone had masked agendas that were wrapped in deceit, hatred, and rejection. I would push away anyone who spoke kindly of me. After being given sincere compliments and words of encouragement, I instantly became defensive. I didn't know how to receive pleasant words from others. The major problem between their compliments and my views was me. I had various inward feelings in my mind that were harsh and horrific. Those beliefs caused me to live from a place of deep insecurities, believing that in order to achieve greatness, I needed an entirely different body.

I couldn't imagine God calling and using me. At one point of my life, I remember praying and asking God to make me another person. I prayed that God would specifically alter things about my appearance that would make me unrecognizable. I didn't know why I felt this way; I simply knew that any association of what I thought made me who I was had to go! Looking back, I feel embarrassed that I could be in such a dark place toward myself. Applying the principle of conviction has caused me to become more transparent about my areas of deliverance.

I believed I couldn't get opulence in my own skin; I had the illusion that I was nothing, and nothing I would be. First things first, John 3:16 says, "For God so loved the world, that he gave his only begotten Son, that whosoever believeth in him should not perish, but have everlasting life." The first thing I had to do was accept the fact that God loves me. I didn't have the ability in times past to love myself, so I had to learn about God's love toward me. If I was going to live a saved and set-apart life, I had to accept the love of Christ. It was very difficult at first because to accept Jesus, I had to accept myself.

Now, I am free from the bondage of self-loathing, which is self-hatred. I was convicted and freed through Jesus Christ and by the Word of God. John 8:36 says, "If the Son therefore shall make you free, ye shall be free indeed." Furthermore, everything I hated about myself was something someone else told me. Someone once told me I was too tall; well, I was a five-year-old kid and had no control over my DNA makeup. I couldn't jump back into my mother's womb and change the dynamics of my appearance! Nevertheless, I hated being tall. I was told that I was too skinny, so I hated being skinny. Another said I had big feet and big hands. There was always something wrong with me to someone else. Everything people said about me was what I hated about myself. I was convicted within my own conscious to start a personal exodus; I began to come out of the place of self-loathing.

One day I was sitting in prayer, and as I prayed and worshipped God, He began to speak to me. "Do not tell Me anything else about what they say unless you're talking about the scriptures. You can tell Me what scriptures says about you but not what man says about you." I began crying because for so long, I gave authority to those who do not have the power to take my breath nor a heaven or hell to put me in.

I made a declaration that I would love myself no matter what. I declared that I would never talk about myself in a negative way again. I gave up the fallacy that I was nothing, and I held on to the truth that I am more than a conqueror. I encourage you to make a declaration against your negative mindset and say, "I am who and what God says I am! I am more than the negative thoughts—I think! I am more than what they say, and I am all of what God says!" Disagree with everything negative that your mind throws at you and love yourself.

The Word of God was cutting through that bubble vortex of other people's words in which I was entrapped. I didn't rest under my self-loathing bulldozer any longer. I took small steps to liking myself. The steps began small and then grew larger. I began to love myself after a while. The self-loathing didn't happen overnight, so it took mass amounts of time to intentionally embrace loving myself. Finally the abuse stopped, and I realized I would not allow anyone else nor myself to hurt me anymore. I quickly recognized areas of addressment so that I didn't spiral downward or relapse in my new-found self-love.

I went on dates with myself. I smiled and winked at myself. I knew to whom I belonged. I fell in love with love, and that's God! I began to smile more. I began to walk tall and persevere. I didn't feel inferior to my negative thoughts and insecurities any longer. I was able to look in the mirror and smile. Of course, it took practice and many scriptures, but God brought me through it. I realized that I was the righteousness of God. I could hold my head up because what others said didn't matter anymore—it was what God said! I realized the hatred I embodied toward myself started from the seed of another's dislike or hate. Someone else planted the seed, but I kept it watered and nourished.

I say to everyone who will listen: Please, love yourself. Don't speak negative words over your life. Proverbs 18:21 says, "Death and life are in the power of the tongue: and they that love it shall eat the fruit thereof." I learned to counterattack self-loathing by walking in the freedom that my conviction to love myself brought me. When people called me tall, I'd say, "Thank you for looking up to me." I began to wear high-heeled shoes and walk tall wherever I went. When people called me skinny, I said, "I am preparing now for a potential midlife spread." I no longer tried to eat every unhealthy food I saw just to put on weight so I wasn't called skinny.

When people called me Bigfoot, I said, "They are necessary for the ground I must cover while laboring in the vineyard. God has a great assignment for me, and I must walk worthy of my calling." When they laughed at my hands, I said, "They are the right size for such a great anointing I must carry. As God uses me as a willing vessel to work in His vineyard and lay hands on the sick, and they recover, I must have big hands for great power to flow through them from God." I noticed my daily attitude toward myself had changed for my good. The things I once internalized had began to break!

It isn't easy to make this type of change, especially when it's been carried throughout our lives, but if we really have a heart to submit the issue to God for change, He will respond with change. No matter what it looks like or sounds like, do not talk yourself into a negative vortex. Do not feed yourself the lies saying you can't make it, because you can make it! Do not feed yourself the lies saying you're not good enough, because you are good enough! Do not feed yourself the lies saying you are nothing, because you are something! Do not feed yourself the lies saying don't love yourself, because you are loved! God thought you were worth the life of his Son, Jesus Christ. Love no matter what!

Write yourself a note of encouragement for seven consecutive days. Whether you use scrap paper, a notebook or journal paper, or a napkin, just write an encouraging note!

Tell yourself, "I will love myself more today!" It's a declaration and a prophecy over your own life. My prayer is that self-love becomes a priority and that you begin to love yourself more, starting today!

Chapter 5

LOVE

Another very personal conviction I have is love. I grew to understand that true and pure love is perfected overtime but requires God. But why was I so afraid of love? For starters, I was afraid to love myself and others out of fear. The anxiety I felt at the thought of loving and being vulnerable was intense. I was fearful that things would go wrong—or even right. My feelings about love were very unconventional and were warped within vast preexisting circumstances and conditions.

I searched for love at a very young age. And yes, I said I searched. During that stage of my life, I believed the love I yearned for would magically appear. I defended anything that fit my warped vision of love. It was foolish of me to believe that I could have something so serious as a broken and hurting child! I mean, how do you attempt to pursue a relationship in any way without the fundamentals of that which you're seeking? But I had so much turmoil in my life that I believed I could conquer this conquest like a mature and secure adult. Instead, I was tossed deeper into a place that I could not climb out of.

I had so many areas of insecurities that I allowed my finite mind to believe that love came from people just saying they loved you. Or better yet, those who stressed a strong desire to have sex. I had many misconceptions of love and often allowed my misconceptions to play out in my life. My ignorance and limited exposure to love corrupted many early years of dating in my life. Due to the limited love I felt, I began shielding myself and avoiding any potentially healthy, lasting, loving relationships.

I would decline the possibility of any future relationships becoming serious, growing, or flourishing into anything more than someone I was kicking it with. I was so mixed up that I didn't recognize whether true love was being showered on me or whether I was simply having a moment of practice. I was preoccupied and too busy entertaining the concept of what I thought a relationship looked like in my mind. It was better to me to live out the fictional story I had created than to pick the wrong guy and be hurt, or even pick someone who was right and get hurt. I had a horrible and reckless pattern concerning love, and I didn't realize it until I experienced the conviction of God's love as He moved strongly in my life. I had a rough upbringing and rationalized whether God or anyone else really loved me.

The majority of the time, something was chaotic and out of place in my life, so why should I believe in an inevitable failure called love? That was my personal perspective. I could never face myself looking in the mirror, so why try to look at love? The ones who were supposed to protect me did the most hurt, so why see normalcy in what I knew was an abnormality? It was clear to me that I didn't truly love myself or possess the ability to truly love others, so how could God love me? I was insecure in being loved and loving others.

A few people encouraged me to read Romans 5:8, "But God commendeth his love toward us, in that, while we were yet sinners, Christ died for us." But when I read it, there was no revelation nor conviction for me at the time. Therefore I still didn't believe in true love. I had too many hardships in past relationships with people. It was extremely rocky and filled with anguish and disappointments, so I didn't have an expectation of hope for anything else. I didn't want anyone, anywhere, at any time trying to love me, and I meant that from the depths of my heart.

I knew there was a form of love that gave necessities, but the way it was expressed from the heart in my life was far from affectionate. When God sent people to tell me that He loves me, I doubted it. But finding out I was pregnant was the beginning of my true conviction to love. I verbalized my love for God and people, and I was preaching, teaching, and praying but I didn't understand why I was still uneasy about letting go to love in its freedom. I had no experience in love's purity and truthfulness in my life.

With all that I knew about love, I gave too much of its power to others to satisfy me. Therefore, my thoughts were not centered on the source of love. If our minds become tainted with the belief that love is not real or obtainable, the enemy will win. In the book of 1 John 4:7 it says, "Beloved, let us love one another: for love is of God; and every one that loveth is born of God, and knoweth God." If the enemy can make us believe, even for a second, that love is an unattainable fantasy, then we could reject love. Love is God!

What I was most convicted about was me being the one rejecting the love of God. Experiencing trials, hurt, and pain over periods of my life overshadowed the very existence of God's undying and never-ending love toward me. The enemy convinced me that God didn't love me because He allowed hurt and pain to enter my life, so I resisted God. I know one may have experienced some very hurtful things from mothers, fathers, sisters, and brothers, but God is still love.

Constant meditation and focus on 1 Corinthians 13 in its entirety helped me in total deliverance and conviction, acceptance and triumph in receiving, and showing and applying the love of God in my life. In that scripture, I learned the true intent of love and had a model of what I was and was not doing concerning love. I was able to reflect on what I believed and what was true about love. I soon realized the importance of love because it is God's, and it's a direct reflection of Him! I was convicted within my own conscious by the scriptures. It was evident that all that I thought was something was nothing without the expression of love.

Please understand that I absolutely love the Word of God I love working in the kingdom of God and being a blessing to His people. I was saved, sanctified, Holy Ghost filled, and not delivered! I hadn't received true love for my life due to various insecurities and misconceptions. God used Scripture for me to receive an awakening because I relied on them as my blueprint for daily living and coping with life's challenges. I finally accepted revelation on the love of God that spreads abroad, and I was delivered.

God blessed me with the furtherance of this openness to love through my pregnancy. I received revelation and understanding over a nine-month period of my life as I carried my baby girl. She shared the inside of me, and I didn't want her to be in distress or rejected under any situation! I faced the root of my disconnection with love and disagreed with it. I fought hard because I knew in my heart that if I didn't change for real, my baby girl would suffer. I didn't want my daughter to inherit any absence of love in any way. I spoke love over her every day as she grew within me.

The duration of being pregnant was teaching, preparing,

and perfecting love in me prior to her arrival. Glory to God, my daughter has never experienced a lack of love. If anything, she gets away with most things. I do realize the odds of me loving her like I do are all because of God. There is no way I can say it was me; had God not spoken to me as soon as the stick said positive, our lives could have been much different. I believe God loves me so much because he wanted me to parent His daughter with an abundance of love.

Usually when you don't love yourself, there's not much that you do love. "I love you" was one of the most difficult and stressful things for me to say. Yet it was natural to say to my daughter once I became a mother. I knew as I carried her in my womb that I would love her more than anything. I wasn't afraid of the thought of loving her. I had begun the process of real love toward myself, so I was enamored of her and hadn't met her personally. It wasn't until God blessed me with a baby that I knew I could love unconditionally. Even after I had given birth and begun to fulfill the duty of motherhood, I understood that God would continue to perfect my love for her over time. In 1 John 4:12b it says, "If we love one another, God dwelleth in us, and His love is perfected in us." We both have benefited from the freedom that the conviction of love brought!

We must choose love and allow God to love us as only He can. When we allow the conviction of God's love to overtake us, then we can experience, see, feel, and understand how much He truly loves us. It wasn't until after I was freed from life's rejections that I was no longer fearful or restraining love, and I was released to love. I have a firm conviction that I am free to love and be loved! I know that love is surrounding me every day. As I see the trees blow in the wind, I am constantly reminded of the positivity of God's love.

It doesn't matter what anyone says; love is not abusive or reckless. Love does not cost you everything that you have, including your identity. Love does not reassure low places and areas of insecurities. Love lifts a standard within you! Love is such a sacred word; its manifestation can turn the wicked into innocent and the unjust into just. Love doesn't intentionally set up stumbling blocks for others. Love is working at something to achieve more. Love is standing still, steadfast and unmovable, in wait for the prize. Love is depending on a greater cause. Love is refreshing and understanding. Furthermore, love is not misleading. Because God is love! I pray this prayer of love over my life, and I pray this for you right now.

Father, thank You for Your lovingkindness that's better than life toward us. Father, I ask that You strengthen our minds and console our hearts. Father, in every area of hurt that we've experienced that has turned us away from love, please help us. Father, I'm asking You to heal our hearts and give us peace in our minds. Stir up the love within us. Love is a fruit of the spirit, and we are praying for its operation within us. For every failed relationship, every source of rejection, every feeling of abandonment, every root of bitterness, and every seed of discord where love should prevail, we surrender it all to You, Father. Teach us how to love You, ourselves, our families, our friends, our communities, and our enemies. Perfect the measure of love within us. You didn't have to love us, but You did, so increase our faith and ability to love. In Jesus's name, amen.

Chapter 6

FORGIVENESS

Having a conviction of forgiveness can be challenging. When people hurt you so badly that you want to hurt them, the last thing you're thinking about is forgiveness. Scripture says in Matthew 6:15 (NIV), "But if you do not forgive others their sins, your Father will not forgive your sins." Do you love yourself enough to make the choice to forgive? You are the only person who can make it! When I think about forgiveness, I think about Jesus on the cross.

Jesus set the unprecedented example of forgiveness that no other can measure. While Jesus hung from a tree after having the beard ripped off his face; being mocked, scorned, bruised, beaten, and whipped; having his skin lacerated; being spat upon, wounded, and bleeding while on the cross dying, He yet considered our future and knew we'd need forgiveness!

He knew His death would cover all of our transgressions and iniquities if we repent and receive forgiveness through Him.

Jesus didn't commend Himself back to God until He asked God, His Father, to forgive the very people who "thought" they were killing him. Luke 23:34a says, "Then said Jesus, Father, forgive them; for they know not what they do." This scripture is very powerful and I received illumination after reading the passage. Jesus, who is the Word made flesh, could not die and sow a seed of unforgiveness. The seeds that are sown will manifest a harvest at some point. How could we then come to God for forgiveness if we didn't witness the only way to God being fulfilled in every area through the death, burial, and resurrection of Jesus Christ? Unforgiveness could not be planted, or it would have been impossible for us to be forgiven. Thank You, Jesus Christ, for being the illustration we should aspire to be like concerning forgiveness!

When Jesus taught the parables of the sower in Mark 4:14, He said, "The sower soweth the word." He's the sower and the Word! It's such an amazing concept because God's Word is true. Jesus demonstrated such a powerful working to all that could see and hear Him before His death. Jesus had planned all along to go down deep to take in hand the keys that would free us, and there was no way unforgiveness was going to get in the way of that. Jesus is the bridge that we have to connect us to our Father through repentance. When we repent, we're requesting forgiveness along with speaking, receiving, accepting, believing, and turning from a life of sin. Jesus asked His Father to forgive the guilty even in the midst of their ignorance, just as God the Father forgives us if we ask in the midst of our ignorance. Wow, Jesus did come that we all might be free!

Jesus also included forgiveness in His instruction on how to pray in Matthew 6:12, "And forgive us our debts, as we forgive our debtors." We forgive because we are forgiven. As I began to experience my personal forgiveness journey, I realized that the process involved healing as well as the freewill choice to forgive. It takes humility, patience, and meekness to accept the conviction of forgiveness.

The choice to forgive is not for the faint at heart. Remember, conviction is to stand on a principle of your beliefs, even when it's not popular. Prayerfully, you will purpose within your heart to adopt a true and pure conviction to forgive, meaning no matter who, what, when, where, why, or how, you will forgive! You must look beyond all personal emotions and feelings to overcome the unwillingness to forgive. I understand it is difficult, but forgiving is best because it's God's Word fulfilled in your life.

There was a time when I could hold a grudge until the day of our soon coming king. I wouldn't let an ant walk on my feet without having a long-standing beef. Nevertheless, I did not forgive, and when I did, I side-eyed people for a long time afterward. I didn't realize how horrible it was to not forgive people until I was convicted. Learning to truly forgive may take some time and is a process, but your freedom that comes afterward is worth the focus. In this case, I didn't see freedom of forgiveness coming either—it smacked me in the face!

In my heart, I had gotten rid of everything done to me that wasn't good. To my defense, I had moved the hurt out of my mind but didn't realize it took up residency in my heart. I had to navigate through some very public and hurtful situations in my life. I applied myself to love in very intimate and personal ways only to be hurt and disappointed. I know what it's like to experience devastating circumstances in a loving and committed relationship. I know what betrayal in its ugliest form can do to the heart and mind when you are simply focused on loving another person appropriately for the journey. I have received some shocks that shook me to my core while knocking the wind out of me. There are times I grappled to understand what I may have done to cause such heart-wrenching unfaithfulness. Yet I found a way to truly forgive with my heart and move on.

Honestly, forgiving those who hurt me was one of the most difficult challenges I faced, next to genuinely loving myself. I thought I had forgiven people many times but was surprised to experience I hadn't. The thoughts that surfaced once I saw them sometimes frightened me. Upon that awareness, I started to make myself uncomfortable with my thoughts. At that moment, I realized that my heart was yet bitter, and I really hadn't forgiven them at all.

I began to seek God for total deliverance, healing, and freedom from my oppressor. The Lord showed me that rejecting forgiveness tied me to the past and caused a hindrance in me being fully propelled into my future. Ultimately, I was the oppressor because I wouldn't allow true forgiveness to flow. I had to forgive others and forgive myself too. As usual, I began to pile every failure on me. I abused myself by self-blaming and questioning my character. I declared that everything was my fault, even if it wasn't. I didn't acknowledge any of the hurt that was done to me. I had tunnel vision and was on the path of destruction.

One day the Lord sent one of my sisters in Christ to minister to me about forgiveness. I was puzzled and thought, *Lord, what now?* I had spent so much time blaming myself for everything that happened in my life that I didn't see the need to forgive anyone because I had absorbed all the blame. I worked daily to sort through the thought to forgive and to whom that may apply. I wanted to be sure in my mind and heart that I was free from unforgiveness. I didn't want to just forgive exes—I wanted the freedom to forgive family, friends, enemies, and anyone whom I had an offence with, whether I knew it or not. Including forgiving myself!

One of the biggest points of forgiveness I learned is that forgiveness doesn't have a look. My analogy of forgiving was everyone sitting at a treaty table and signing a document of forgiveness. Clearly, I was wrong because forgiveness is such a heart matter. People can't know your true intentions of forgiveness unless you tell them. It's an inward job that displays outwardly. I can honestly say I no longer dance with the heaviness of unforgiveness. Whether I'm at fault or not, whether there is an offence or not, my choice is to forgive!

I made up in my heart that enough was enough, and the Lord began to minister directly to my heart. He prepared a plan of action for me to walk into the freedom of forgiveness. I no longer wanted unforgiveness, bitterness, hatred, animosity, guilt, resentment, and self-torment choking out the attributes of Christ. I wanted people to see the fruit of the spirit being displayed and operating in my life.

My desire was to put to death everything contrary to God's Word that caused me to remain engulfed in unforgiveness. God gave me four actions to exercise to stay free in my mind. But before we go into those, I want you to search your heart and locate the place that has harbored unforgiveness or a lack of forgiveness within you. When you arrive at that destination, look for a root. When you establish the root, speak to it, disagree with it, and declare that it will no longer have rule over you. Do not allow unforgiveness to sit at the seat of your emotions. Then you should pray this prayer of forgiveness.

Lord, even now, I repent of any offence I've held against Your people. I ask You to open my spiritual eyes to the pathway of forgiveness. I ask You to open the eyes of my heart and my mind and begin the conviction process of forgiveness. Forgive my trespasses as I forgive those who trespassed against me. Stir up conscious compassion, grace, and mercy toward others. In Jesus's name, amen.

Chapter 7

LET GO

I've forgiven them—now what? It's time for some action, so let go!

PLAN OF ACTION

1st: Forgive by choice … The choices we make are very powerful! Forgiveness is not an emotion; it's a choice and YOU are the ONLY person that can choose to forgive! Forgiveness is not done because you are weak, it's done because you love yourself enough to pursue freedom. Choose you this day to give yourself the gift of forgiveness. You need to release that person so that God can work on them and you too!

There are somethings being withheld due to the refusal of forgiveness. Stop trying to hold people hostage in bondage,

God is NOT pleased! Ultimately, you're only binding yourself! Every time that person is around, you're the one uncomfortable and awkward. You're the one that has the ungodly thoughts. You're the one with no peace of being settled.

The only person bound is the one practicing unforgiveness. Forgiveness can be hard, but somebody must do it! Forgive yourself, release yourself, love yourself, encourage yourself, believe in yourself and tell yourself I can make it! You can do it; you are the righteousness of God! You are forgiven and possess the ability to forgive others! Make forgiveness your first choice.

2nd: This next one is the MOST difficult ... LET IT GO! There is a difference between forgetting and letting it go. God allows us to forgive but we don't forget. There are some situations when God will cause us to forget something as we're healing and pressing to forgive with conviction. Generally, only God has the constant power and authority to forgive and forget. We do however have the power to forgive then choose to let it go.

Stop tormenting yourself about what they did and if they deserve your forgiveness. Now, I DO UNDERSTAND that some things people have done or said to you, make it difficult to forgive or let it go. The beauty of God is that we're not alone in this feeling. There is nothing we have to do in our own strength. We have a helper in The Holy Spirit! It is ONLY through my relationship with The Trinity that I am steadfast in forgiveness. If you don't believe me, let me explain, I experienced firsthand dealing with the "but syndrome". What is the "but syndrome", it's personal justification and judgement of whether or not somebody should be forgiven.

"But they mistreated me, but they hurt me, but they abused me, but they disrespected me, but they hit me, but they spat on me, but they hated me, but they neglected me, but they molested me, but they cheated on me, but they abandoned me, but they stole from me, but they manipulated me, but they killed my family/friend, but they used me, but they mistreated the kids, but they played mental games with me, but they were discriminative, but they were racist towards me, but they are a rapist, but they are an awful person, but-but-but they don't deserve forgiveness or for me to EVER let what "they" did go!"

BUT then I heard the Word of The Lord say, *"And such were some of you: but ye are washed, but ye are sanctified, but ye are justified in the name of the Lord Jesus, and by the Spirit of our God."* Took me by surprise and I immediately went to search the word and found it in 1 Corinthians 6:11. I felt rebuked because I should never think so highly of self that I would look down on someone else. It is ONLY through the redemptive work of the blood of Jesus that was shed for the remission of sin that allows us to be forgiven. God loved us so much that He let his son Jesus step down out of heaven, to die, so that we might have a chance to live. We have no right to hold hatred, resentment, unforgiveness, oughts' and offences in our hearts towards our brothers/sisters but declaring we love God. I get it, it doesn't make sense a times but God is sovereign and answers to no one.

If your profession is not Christ, forgiveness is yet a healthier option for you! Holding on to hurt keeps you bound while others are living their lives. Nobody is perfect in this earth; everyone makes mistakes or bad choices. Forgiveness is for you, not them! If you believe you hold that much power over someone to keep them bound to their past, you are no different than them. Forgiveness is exercised as a sign of remarkable love, unforgiveness fuels hate.

Let go of the hate by the choice to let go of the offense. Again, somethings do take time and the human mind does not always forget but I entreat you to let it go. It may require some adjustments, time and maybe talking it out with someone but you are always worth your freedom! Think about this, you can't fully reach the 6 ft. in front of you, grabbing at the 3ft behind you. Letting go spearheads the freedom to move forward. Letting go simply says, all the things attached to what you did, I will no longer hold those with such prevalence in my life. You don't have to walk extremely close to that person as a choice, but if or when you see them, and you're not bound by the past feelings, you have freed yourself my friend!

Your clear future is ahead of you! God has promised you

some things and your obedience to His Word is required to reach your fullness. Let it go because you can't get new things with the old mindset; just as you shouldn't pour new wine into old bottles. God is calling you higher! It's your future happiness and you can't give it up! Generational chains of unforgiveness are broken with you! The Lord will give you strength so exercise faith to forgive and let go!

3rd: Faith to forgive ... Some things that have been done to us have taken root and grew into a 30ft Mulberry Tree with bitter red berries! We want our refreshingly sweet fruit back! Faith is when we trust that God's judgement is more than enough. We release people by faith so that we're not found guilty of condemning people to hell.

In Luke chapter 17, Jesus was teaching his disciples on forgiveness. He gave precise instructions on how many times to forgive a person of the same offence in the same day if they repent to them. Knowing that was a bit more than they could do within their own strength, the apostles asked Jesus to increase their faith. I noticed something significant about this teaching. In the beginning of the chapter, the men were acknowledged as disciples but as soon as they asked for increased faith to forgive to such an extent, they were referred to as apostles.

Faith is a key essential to elevation. Quite frankly, to forgive on another level, our faith must grow to another level! Then we will think on another level and reach towards another level. Oftentimes, we think of faith as a means of receiving something. Many people exercise faith for new cars, homes, children, etc. but faith to forgive could go unnoticed. Faith is a powerful spiritual weapon! It is a shield to keep our bodies covered from fiery arrows in an attack. If we exercise true faith, we will exemplify the power to forgive just as Jesus taught! Mountains can be moved with faith the size of a mustard seed. There is also faith that will cause all things to be possible. The conviction and principle of true forgiveness is possible by faith.

4th: Forgive with your heart … Forgiveness is with the heart not the mind. In Matthew 18:35 Jesus said, *"So likewise shall my heavenly Father do also unto you, if ye from your hearts forgive not everyone his brother their trespasses."* Again, Jesus is teaching us that EVERYONE deserved to be forgiven because despite our status, we all had to be forgiven of our sins! Forgiveness is a heart condition, and our hearts are worth guarding and protecting!

It's understandable to guard against hurtful situations or circumstances but we shouldn't hate and choose not to forgive because of it. No matter what "they" do or did, you do what's right because you will have to give a personal account of your behavior. Will you allow the person that has given you the most hurt on earth, be the reason why you don't hear well done? The reality is, no one should have that much power over you. Forgive with your heart so when you see them, you're not trying to doge them and go in the opposite direction. Pray for discernment on how to handle God's people, remember, everyone had to be forgiven, including you.

Chapter 8

FEAR

Failure is obtained 100 percent of the time if that's all you believe you'll achieve because of fear. Fear will attempt to overtake the mind of those it inhabits! Having a sound mind is significant in the refusal to fear the things of life. One of my absolute favorite scriptures is 2 Timothy 1:7, "For God hath not given us the spirit of fear; but of power and, and of love, and of a sound mind." There is something paralyzing about fear within the mindset.

Fear penetrates places that are only imaginable in our worst nightmares. It consumes our lives and thoughts and disrupts the healthy patterns of logical thinking. Oftentimes people will point out characteristics of fear within you because it's the fruit you're bearing. Stabilizing fear is not the answer because we develop a systematic response to fear causing the development of a happy medium of blissful tolerance.

Fear is so strong that it counteracts faith, which is one of two important attributes necessary to please God and receive salvation through repentance. Fear in the sense of fight, flight, or adrenaline rush is necessary. But the fear that stops you from going to the store due to a local news story is unacceptable. We must foil fear and all its siblings! If the process of conviction can set us free from fear, then why are we still enslaved?

Holding on to the past due to the fear of stepping into your future will lead to destruction. As you may have noticed throughout this book, without the principle of conviction, I would have continued to struggle in various areas of my life. Some of my most intimate personal freedoms are written within this book. There were many times I allowed my thoughts to destroy my life because I was fearful of my weaknesses and being exposed. I am called to lead, but I wouldn't move because I didn't want my shortcomings and areas needing deliverance to be known or considered by anyone.

I lost valuable years and time, but thank God, He is the keeper of time! If you're reading this, you still have time to consciously decide that fear will not run your life.

1 John 4:18 (NIV) says, "There is no fear in love. But perfect love drives out fear, because fear has to do with

punishment. The one who fears is not made perfect in love." At one period in my life, I did not have the ability to love myself or others because I operated solely in fear. I remember being terrified to love with my heart, thus causing me to love at a heart's distance.

I allowed love to get close enough for me to care a little, never having intentions of anything more because I was fearful of being hurt. There were things, words, and life events that caused me to fear. Ultimately, I wanted to be delivered and freed from fear. I had a false depiction of what fear looked like. Monsters, scary movies, and spooky dark places were my perceptions of fear. That was definitely not the right thought regarding fear!

However, there is a fear that can bring knowledge, and that's a fear of God. Would you look at that? The very thing that separated me from love had a component that was needed to receive knowledge. I had no awareness that while I digested mine and the enemies-imposed fear, I spewed out the fear of the Lord due to lack of knowledge. I would never want to reject the knowledge of God, so I began to cooperate with the move of God through conviction. I began to stand up to the fear that was tormenting my thoughts. I am constantly working daily to walk in continuous deliverance and conviction against fear.

Ambitions on releasing this book was a conquest over fear for me. I must admit there is a constant battle of fear. You must be careful and on alert regarding fear. Sometimes you don't recognize it until you're dealing with it face-to-face, seeing a red light when God has given the green light! As long as you stand on the freedom to move as God gives and not rest in the valley of fear, you have the victory!

God had given me the green light to write and publish this book. The thoughts and information within me had to come out for the masses to evaluate. I was petrified to open myself up to others by voluntarily inviting them into my life to give opinions and reviews. It wasn't someone else's thoughts to be evaluated; they were mine. I am the one responsible for the customer service scores. The responsibility to sell my brand, ideas, and thoughts, leaving me vulnerable to what others might say, was fearful to me.

Thanks be to God that I have a constructive outlook on what other people say. I know how to filter through what's fruitful and what's unfruitful. I have a healthier way of thinking, and I'm no longer afraid to embrace who I am or to make a difference in the world without fear. Of course, there are still the natural points of fight or flight, but not fear! I utilize the Word of God and testimonies of overcomers to combat falling back into being fearful.

If you're battling fear and moving into your stance of conviction, it takes some work. There are many scriptures on which I had to constantly meditate. As I grew and developed in overcoming fear and maintaining a conviction of fear, I went through some very rough valleys. The enemy was always fighting to keep me stagnate. Once fear is rooted, many goals and dreams are pushed aside.

Fear is a learned behavior with contributing factors from our past experiences and feelings. If faced with a situation that feels familiar or seems similar to a hard place, we often don't advance forward. That's no longer the enemy blocking you—you yourself are unwilling to pursue. Let's completely stomp out fear in our lives so that we can help someone else. The conviction of fear truly frees you from habits of the past.

No more fear, and no more holding back on your dreams! The enemy is always trying to replicate things of God. We've already established that fearing the Lord is the starting point of knowledge. That knowledge may lead to repentance to God, which leads to salvation. There are over five hundred Bible scriptures with the word *fear*, and they're not all a place of defeat, doom, or gloom. There's only one true defeat in fear, and that's an eternal life without accepting Christ as your personal Lord and Savior.

> But I'll tell you whom to fear. Fear God, who has the power to kill you and then throw you into hell. Yes, he's the one to fear. (Luke 12:5 NLT)

Chapter 9

‡‑o‑o‑o‑o‑o‑o‑o‑o‑o‑o‑o‑o‑o‑o‑o‑o‑o‑o‑o‑o‑o‑o‑o‑o‑o‑o‑o‑o‑o‑o‑o‑o‑o‑o‑o‑o‑o‑o‑‡

THINK RIGHT

A positive thinking process is just as important to our well-being as drinking water. Instability is birthed through the operation of a double mind. James 1:8 says, "A doubleminded man is unstable in all his ways." Our perception of thought weighs heavily on our facts and experiences about life. Wavering between beliefs is one way to be classified as doubleminded. Philippians 2:5 says, "Let this mind be in you, which was also in Christ Jesus."

If the muscle between our ears is poisoned, we will have a challenging time seeing the positivity of life. Personally, I overcomplicated and overanalyzed everything in my thinking approach. When I heard the letter *A*, I was already reciting *Z*. I had no balance in my thinking; it was zero to one hundred in seconds. I was impulsive in my thoughts, even while listening, always looking for what to say next, whether positive or negative (but mostly negative).

While reading, I would insert words and scenarios that were completely contrary to the material I was looking at because I had preexisting scenarios crafted in my mind that led me to function in biased ways. Furthermore, it was very draining to constantly think that way. I began to recall conversations that I had in times past with my family and friends over my lifetime. I was flabbergasted when I came to the realization that over 70 percent of my dialect with them was negative. It was even more alarming that most of my everyday thoughts were too.

I know that seems irrational, but it's the truth. I took notice because one day as I read a very positive and upbeat passage, I kept thinking about *Criminal Minds* scenarios and applying them to what I was reading. Negative and tainted thinking spilled into my daily living, and every day I thought about the worst-case scenarios happening. I didn't verbalize many of these thoughts, but it got to the point that I was weirding myself out. I started asking God what was wrong with my thinking.

What I love about God is that He will always give answers to your questions. I knew in my consciousness that the wrong thinking had to go. I knew for me to face such a blemish about myself, it had to be a move of God! I would never address myself on my thinking; I was already living with it. I knew I wanted to think healthier, and when that change came forth, I would embrace it until breath left my body.

I sought out a life choice for change in my thinking because I was made aware of the negative impact I had exalted in my imaginations. I wanted to have a conviction of right thinking. It's not normal to have a mind that is always looking for the worst to happen. It's not healthy to expound upon a terrible situation and even play out the scenarios that the mind can create.

In the article "For Sound Mental Health, Think Again about Your Thinking," Dr. Noam Shpancer[1] suggests that we should exchange our thinking habits, be it good or bad, with accurate thinking. Here is a part of what he wrote within his article.

> Accurate thinking is important because we know today, through the pioneering work of psychologists such as Albert Ellis, Aaron Beck and others, that your thoughts—the beliefs, interpretations and assumptions you make about yourself and the world around you—can shape your feelings and actions. For example, if a friend passes you by on the street without saying hello,

---

[1] Noam Shpancer, "For Sound Mental Health, Think Again About Your Thinking," Psychology Today (Sussex Publishers, September 17, 2010), https://www.psychologytoday.com/us/blog/insight-therapy/201009/sound-mental-health-think-again-about-your-thinking, 1.

your reaction to that event will depend on how you choose to interpret it. If you come to believe that your friend has intentionally ignored you, then you are likely to feel certain feelings (such as anger, surprise, disappointment, or confusion). Later, when you meet this friend again, you are also likely to behave in certain, perhaps hostile, ways based on your belief that he ignored you on purpose. However, if instead you come to believe that your friend did not notice you passing by, or that he did not recognize you because you had lost weight recently, or that he had lost his eyesight in a terrible accident, then you are likely to feel and behave differently upon your next encounter. The event itself (your friend ignoring you) is not as important to your subsequent feelings and behavior as is your interpretation of the event.

After I had the opportunity to read this article, I began to pray and think about all the relationships I lost because people told me they thought I was acting "some type of way," or maybe I felt the same. It was amazing how much I could relate to the psychological aspect of this article. I remembered a situation arising years ago, and I'll share it now because my testimony now is that I'm free from this type of thinking, but in the past I was out of control in my thoughts.

One day I encountered a situation at work and just couldn't shake the thought of it. I needed to tell someone at that very moment. My matter was of urgency, and someone needed to be there for me, or so I thought. I called eight different people, and no one answered. Automatically my thoughts raced even more because I couldn't reach anyone. I pursued person after person with more anxiousness and excitement after every call. I was thinking all types of things that were against these people's characters.

I couldn't stop being angry and thinking the worse. I was convinced by my own mind that everyone had decided to walk out on me at the same time! I kept telling myself, What are the odds that all the people you would call are unavailable at the same time? That was me justifying my irrational thoughts. And the worst part is in that moment, I remembered people projecting ideologies that their minds thought up against me that hurt in the past. But none of that mattered because my mind was already programmed to think the worse, and I couldn't turn it off.

I went on in this way of thinking for almost an hour, until I heard the voice of God say, "Peace!" I came to myself and was amazed at how angry I had become at people over being unavailable. Right then, God spoke, and I instantly felt the conviction of never wanting to feel like that again. I declared in my mind that no matter what was happening around me, I would stand against breaking up great relationships because of my thinking. I repented and praised God for my freedom through conviction. I knew my consciousness of erratic thinking was over because I felt a peace that I couldn't describe. Of course, I have moments to push back, yet I stand on my conviction to think right.

Now, when I can't reach people for whatever reason, my thoughts are not poisoned. Sometimes I jokingly say they are planning a surprise gathering! for me That may not be accurate thinking, but it is more positive thinking, and it gives me a balance. It gives me an anchor to use in order to slow down and reposition my thoughts. I no longer desire to overanalyze my thinking. I understand the point of accurate thinking, but if I'm always accurate, where does God come in? Trying to be accurate in our own thoughts could desensitize us to God's conviction process because He's always accurate and right, and we're not.

In addition to accurate thinking, Dr. Shpancer posed a process for cognitive reappraisal (an assessment of something or someone again or in a different way)[2] that I fully agree could help those that go through the steps without self-prejudice.

---

[2]   Noam Shpancer, "For Sound Mental Health, Think Again About Your Thinking," Psychology Today (Sussex Publishers, September 17, 2010), https://www.psychologytoday.com/us/blog/insight-therapy/201009/sound-mental-health-think-again-about-your-thinking, 2.

1. Identify your maladaptive thought habits (the automatic thoughts)
2. Generate alternatives to your initial, automatic interpretation
3. Look for evidence regarding which of the thoughts is most likely to be correct
4. Adopt the best, most plausible interpretation

This process is important and necessary because we are instructed by God to examine and sober ourselves. There are things in our control and those that are not. Our designation and posture should include watching over the thinking we allow in our minds. The way we think is in our control, but a completely surrendered lifestyle to Christ allows Him to lead our thoughts. That also contributes to discernment, which allows an insight into things that may or may not be.

We all have thinking habits, and whether they are good, bad, accurate, or indifferent we cannot change our will to think. However, if we stand on the conviction to think right, we can counteract and stand against everything contrary to our freedom to think right. As we work out our bodies and change our eating habits to become healthier, so should we work out our thinking habits to have healthier thinking. For me, poisonous thinking had become a habit, so even after being convicted, delivered, and set free, I still had the responsibility to unlearn the habits of thinking the worst first.

The difference between a good or bad outcome begins with a thought. What we are thinking that goes from mind to heart becomes our motive. If we chose to make a conscious effort to think healthily instead of irrationally, we will have less self-imposed anxiety. That's a personal testimony for me because I had less anxiety after I stopped thinking an entire storyline for someone else. This area of conviction truly changed my life and gave me freedom to trust God with His plan for my life. I can honestly say this required tons of work on my end.

The enemy attempts to keep our minds distracted and busy. Many times we're deceived and caught in the past on repeat, and this can bring us torment. We must recognize and identify the root so that freedom from the torment is gained. The conviction to think right was one of the most difficult areas for me to overcome, but I did it, and you can too. Reposition your thoughts. Reassess your intentions. Consider this: you have more power over your thoughts than you give yourself credit for.

> Finally, believers, whatever is true, whatever is honorable *and* worthy of respect, whatever is right *and* confirmed by God's word, whatever is pure *and* wholesome, whatever is lovely *and* brings peace, whatever is admirable *and* of good repute; if there is any excellence, if there is anything

worthy of praise, think *continually* on these things [center your mind on them, and implant them in your heart]. The things which you have learned and received and heard and seen in me, practice these things [in daily life], and the God [who is the source] of peace *and* well-being will be with you. (Philippians 4:8-9 AMP)

Chapter 10

FAITH

Sometimes we think that a walk of faith is through easy street, but oftentimes we're walking through a valley. Of course, God is there with us but it could feel like we're in an estranged situation. I wanted to take some time and set up my journey of finding a conviction of the gift of faith.

The judge asked me for the last time, "Do you want your maiden name back?" She went on to explain that if I ever changed my mind after the ruling was entered, I would have to pay over three hundred dollars or file a motion to get my name back. She stressed to avoid that cost and additional court proceedings and fees, I should speak now, or I would incur the inconvenience later. With so many thoughts and emotions running through my mind and heart, I was clear of one thing: my baby girl asked me to keep her last name after the divorce, and I wanted to be faithful in that desire to her.

I didn't want my daughter to feel the need to explain why she and her mother had different last names. She was already hurt by the decision of her parents, and I didn't want to add any additional heartache. With that settled in my heart, I kept my married name and answered, "I will keep my married name, Your Honor."

After that final decision, my mind was screaming into both of my ears, "Why would you do that? You're no longer with that man. What if you meet someone, and you still have his last name?" It took days before I could shut up my mind. The major problem was five months prior to that, I was led expressly by God to step out on faith and resign from a job I had held for ten years. I was uncertain about how this dramatic change would impact my new norm of living as a single parent. Yet I trusted God by faith because He told me that I had to go on a faith walk so my faith in Him could go to a level above what I could imagine. There was a marathon happening in my life with questions running through my head.

All I knew was I was losing my husband, my house, my dog, my picket fence, and my dignity. And now, Lord, You said to give up my job? I was livid, full of emotions swimming throughout my soul while my heart was plastered on my sleeve. I couldn't understand why God would say to resign at a time like this. I wrestled the entire month of December wondering why God was requiring such a crazy thing of me. Honestly, I felt foolish to even think about it, and people around me already knew what I was facing.

The magnitude of how much my life had taken a shift was overwhelming. There was a fight happening within me to secure my own means of support while God was trying to teach me to have more faith in Him. I had a baby girl to see to as a single mother, and income was definitely the way to do that, or so I felt. The day was upon me, and I handed in my two weeks' notice to my employer in obedience to God. My branch manager at the time was completely shocked, and I was too! But I kept moving forward because my faith was in God and not what I saw with my eyes.

During this time, I wasn't a babe in Christ, but I was new to walking in faith and total submission to God. I had made up in my heart, "Not my will but God's will be done in my life." There were many things that God had stripped me from, and it was a good feeling as long as I felt comfortable. My baby girl had just turned seven years old and was entering a season that she never knew before, with one parent daily in our household. It seemed as if everything that I knew was being shaken, and it was.

I was walking by faith and not by sight in a real-life way. On my last day of physically working, I typed up a grand e-mail. Many complimented the contents, but after I walked away that day, I couldn't remember what I had written. At the time of my departure, I would've been classified as middle class. I had worked long enough to receive a pension, and I had a 401(k) savings plan. I kept questioning this walk and began to lose hope. My manager kept asking me to reconsider, but I kept it moving, thinking I must obey God. I was now entering the realms of a stay-at-home mom pursuing my first degree and taking care of my daughter who was overflowing with questions.

The first two months were horrible/ None of the money sources I was supposed to receive came in. I was without funds. I applied for public assistance and was denied! I was furious with that denial after paying into the system since I had been a teenager working. Let's just say God birthed something special in me with that denial. Moving on, I immediately questioned, "What is this, God? Hands down, this is awful. It's not just my life here—I have this little daughter to take care of. This has been the worst two months ever!"

I was borrowing money and asking close family and friends for help until my funds were released. I felt ashamed and foolish at the same time. Then one day as my face was soaked with tears, I grabbed my Bible, and it fell on Romans 8:24–28, "For we are saved by hope: but hope that is seen is not hope: for what a man seeth, why doth he yet hope for? But if we hope for that we see not, then do we with patience wait for it. Likewise the Spirit also helpeth our infirmities: for we know not what we should pray for as we ought: but the Spirit itself maketh intercession for us with groanings which cannot be uttered. And he that searcheth the hearts knoweth what is the mind of the Spirit, because he maketh intercession for the saints according to the will of God. And we know that all things work together for good to them that love God, to them who are the called according to his purpose."

I received the conviction straightway! I started encouraging myself. I didn't realize that in order to have faith, I actually had to have hope that God would answer by faith. Let that sink in! I was telling people about the journey and the process, but God knew I wasn't walking it out in real time. Better yet, I wasn't even on the real pathway.

Honestly, in the beginning, before the last day of work, it felt good to talk about being called to a faith walk. Real-life situations require real faith! I was patty-caking God, and He wasn't pleased, so I had to experience that good ol' on-the-job training. The difference was I didn't have all of the prerequisites, and I hadn't considered a conviction of faith at that point. I learned how to trust God no matter what, and that ignited the fire of my conviction of faith.

The more I declared all things were working together for my good, the more things begin to turn around for me. I would like to put this disclaimer out there: things did not change overnight. But I will fast-forward and testify that God took care of my daughter and me for two and a half years. I made more money in those years that I was unemployed than I ever had while employed. I filed my taxes each year as if I had been working full-time during those years.

As a matter of fact, the IRS sent me a check for over two thousand dollars with interest because they had underpaid me. The greatest principle I learned in establishing a conviction of faith in God was to keep my hope in completely trusting Him and surrendering to His will. In the beginning, things were shaky for me because my hope, trust and faith in Him were shaky. It was impossible for me to please God because I was offering Him fragmented faith! Scripture really convicted me in my heart and conscious.

Read this about faith in Hebrews 11:1, "Now faith is the substance of things hoped for, the evidence of things not seen." Faith goes beyond our physical senses. Establishing a true conviction of faith is determined by the victories and experiences that God has conquered in our lives. Faith is not tangible, but it's within your heart. You can't see faith, but you can walk by it.

Start with a mustard seed size of faith and then grow from faith to faith. Don't make a habit of complacency. Keep exercising your faith in God until it's not a question whether you'd stand up or back down. Stand on the principle of faith and remain steadfast in your conviction. If you magnify your faith in God, He will be faithful to you.

Without faith, you cannot please God because faith is the

prerequisite for believing God exists. Faith is a very critical point to God, and it yield rewards for your diligence in seeking Him. No matter what it feels or looks like, remember that the more faith you have, the more it compels God to work for you. Walk in and work your faith!

Chapter 11

PRAY

1Thessalonians 5:17 simply says, "Pray without ceasing." In all things pray! Today, I sit at the table to write a chapter that was birthed out of current events. My conviction about prayer is having the confidence to stand and believe in the supernatural power of prayer in the midst of chaos while humbly entreating God in the face of adversity and times of abundance. I believe Jesus when He spoke in Mark 11:24, "Therefore I say unto you, What things soever ye desire, when ye pray, believe that ye receive them, and ye shall have them."

What does it mean to pray? It is the way humanity makes petitions to God or gods. Essentially, this is humanity's way to personally communicate by giving and receiving with God. Prayer can also apply corporately and for many reasons. There are prayers of supplication, thanksgiving, worship, faith, adoration, confessions, strategies, and whatever your intimate thoughts and requests are that you would like to make known to God. Receiving Jesus Christ as your personal Lord and Savior puts you in a prime seat for the rewarding of answered prayers! Jesus assured us in Matthew 21:22, "And all things, whatsoever ye shall ask in prayer, believing, ye shall receive."

We are currently in the midst of the COVID-19 pandemic, the first of this magnitude in modern-day history. There is also a rise of people wanting justice for all people with an emphasis on blacks and colored people. There is a movement, Black Lives Matter, and people from all walks of life are speaking up against systemic racist behaviors, police brutality, and injustice toward people of color within the United States. Both of these current events have caused massive confusion, death, and disbelief, yet I cry out and pray.

As a believer in Jesus Christ, I must admit I have been aggressively challenged in my conviction to pray. Every day, up to four people I knew were dying from the virus for three straight months due to complications of the coronavirus. In addition to that, people whom I love and care for deeply are starting to segregate due to the current racial tensions. The virus has single-handedly shut down the world, and racism and injustice has caused the world to reevaluate the true meaning of "justice for all," exposing the unfair treatment of black men and women.

What better way to say you will truly do something no

matter what, until you do it! My nephew was slated to have a high school prom and graduation this year, but they were canceled due to the virus! He's also attending college, and I am concerned for his safety as a black man. We've gone from one extreme to another, yet I believe prayer will make a difference.

Enough of that. I wanted to begin with circumstances that demonstrates although we pray, adversity will come to challenge what we're praying for to discourage our belief that prayer is the most we can do! We should always pray, as instructed by the Bible, and not faint! This is a biblical principle, but what about when you can't? Do you really want God's will if that means a loved one must pass away? Do we stay silent about racism, hatred, or police brutality against blacks? Do you stand on what you believe, or do you throw in the towel because everything is pressing against every prayer? There are so many questions, but as a believer of Christ, prayer can alter everything.

Let's review a few testimonies that confirm the importance of having a conviction to pray. I'll walk you through some scenarios to see the aftermath of believers in God, praying God's will. These stories aren't "I prayed, and God changed everything right then." There was some fasting, disobedience, running, complaining, and complete drama, but our focus from each story is prayer.

Let's begin with the story of Jonah, which is very popular

because many people know which person of the Holy Bible was swallowed up by a big fish! Yes, it was Jonah, but the most beautiful part of the story is what happened when prayer went forth. This story is powerful and short, but I will focus primarily on the points of prayer throughout the story.

A violent storm was on the horizon, and mariners on a boat were crying out to their gods to be saved while en route to Tarshish. There was a prophet named Jonah onboard who was attempting to flee the presence of God. The shipmaster found Jonah fast asleep and entreated him to call upon his God so they would not perish on the ship. Jonah's response was rather peculiar because he admitted he was the problem and requested to be tossed overboard to elude God's instructions rather than obey. The mariners cried out to God before the fulfillment of Jonah's request and actually made a sacrifice and vows to God after the request was completed.

Notice here that the story actually begins with prayer on the boat! Although Jonah was the specific issue, the men on the boat prayed, and God answered. I don't know whether the men onboard had a conviction to pray, but they knew to do so in the face of a storm. Jonah was tossed overboard, and God had prepared a fish to swallow him. For three days and three nights, Jonah was in the belly of that fish! Then he prayed. His prayer was the way out of the belly of the fish.

The Bible declares that after praying out to God, Jonah's prayer was answered, and God spoke to the fish to release

Jonah on dry land. The fish obeyed God, unlike Jonah the first time. And after he was on dry land, he was finally en route to give the word of God to the inhabitants of Ninevah. After Jonah ran a few days to his purposed destination, he went in with the Word expressly provided by God. Once the people heard the message that destruction was sure to come, a fast and prayer were implemented, and God saw the people on one accord and spared Nineveh from destruction.

Prayer, fasting, obedience, being on one accord, and crying out fervently to God is the most we can do! James 5:16b says, "The effectual fervent prayer of a righteous man availeth much." We have the opportunity to experience much by talking with God in prayer! Here are a couple Old Testament stories from the book of Daniel that display souls being saved through prayer.

There were three Hebrew boys whose names are Shadrach, Meshach, and Abednago. These young men were thrown in a furnace to be burned alive because of their conviction to pray only to God Almighty. The king's decree was that everyone must bow and pray to a pagan god at certain times throughout the day, but the three Hebrew boys did not.

Now, as much as I have adversity in my life, I've never had to face death because of it. I honestly can say no matter what I was facing, I would pray to God—that is my conviction! Daniel also faced death due to praying to God, and I would like to make known that he is another example of having a conviction of prayer. But Daniel's punishment was being cast into a den of lions. The Bible truth is that in both scenarios, God made a way of escape and honored each prayer of His people. God saved them from death!

Our convictions about prayer are rooted in our relationship with God through salvation, believing God by faith, and believing His word, His will, and His plan for our lives without doubt. Thus, convictions give us the boldness to stand firm when we're petitioning God. In the earlier examples, each man believed and prayed with assurance that God would deliver him, and if He didn't, it wasn't because He couldn't!

The quick synopses of these stories showcase biblical accounts of conviction to pray in the face of death. I encourage you to read further and more intensely to glean the richness of the full story and godly wisdom exhibited in each situation. Afterward, examine yourself and determine whether you can identify areas in your spiritual life that are similar to those of Jonah, Shadrach, Meshach, Abednago, and Daniel, and then journal your thoughts.

Now, let's talk about something we all can relate to life as we know it today: praying through a pandemic and chaos! My prayer focus has been intentional and convicting to focus on the will of God and not my emotions. Today, I can admit I have fought through many emotions, even doubt, but I have remained in stance of my conviction to pray. I have fought some very raw thoughts and justifiable anger, disappointment, and rage, but I did not waver in my position to seek God in prayer. I may have had tears flowing and did not know what to say, yet I submitted to God in prayer.

The great thing is when we receive the gift of the Holy Spirit, He makes intercession on our behalf when we don't know what to say. It's amazing how much God, our Father, wants to hear from us that He would provide a way to speak to Him in an unknown tongue. Each one of our conversations is important to Him! This pathway keeps us without an excuse to talk to Him.

Although God is sovereign and can hear a prayer or not, answer a prayer or not, move immediately or not, this doesn't change the fact that He can do all things. We must understand that prayer works, but the results may simply be the will of God and not our preferences being answered. This is the most challenging aspect because during these times, people are skeptical regarding whether prayer works and whether it's an affective answer. I understand prayer is action along with physical actions, but prayer should remain the first action! I pray first for strategies to handle what I'm facing. Whether God has answered or not, I have the blueprint for life in the Holy Bible, and as long as that curriculum is available, I will move forward in my conviction to pray.

Father, in the name of Jesus, please guard the spiritual gateways of everyone who reads this prayer. Lord, dry up all places of torment driven by the adversary to afflict Your people. I pray against sickness, disease, hate, racism, snares, traps, ignorance, familiar spirits, distractions, and anything that impacts the hearts and minds of Your people. I pray that the blood of Jesus covers everyone that is fighting negative, chaotic, corrupt thoughts and thoughts of suicide. I pray that the yokes of bondage be destroyed in Jesus's name. I pray that Your people walk in freedom from this day forward, with no more worry or lack. I am confident that no weapon formed against Your people will prosper and that You will condemn every tongue that rises against them in judgment. I pray that You will dismantle the bands of wickedness troubling Your people, lift heavy burdens, and free the captives. Father, I pray that Your anointing falls on them, even now. I pray for love and peace among all humankind no matter the creed or color. I pray that hearts are strengthened, lifted, and encouraged in Your will and Your way. Thank You for Your Word, which proclaims You will give the oil of joy for mourning, beauty for ashes, and praise for the spirit of heaviness. I pray that all people will choose life and liberty in You. I pray that You will heal, deliver, move upon the consciousness, and convict sin. Father, I know that all things are possible in You because You never fail! For Your people, I pray that You make all things new and provide endurance while propelling them into deeper depths and higher heights. I pray that you will give the faint of heart hope to press on and see what the end is going to be. In Jesus's name, amen.

Epilogue

Self-evaluation can be very difficult. Oftentimes people don't truly consider their behaviors or actions, and they refuse to accept responsibility for things they've done. The most important takeaway from this book is that everyone has different personal convictions, struggles, triumphs, and secrets. I've witnessed people handle others in a rough and aggressive way, and that's their conviction: to tell off a person at the drop of a hat. I've also witnessed others be passive and timid because their conviction is to never cause trouble or pushback.

No matter where you stand in your convictions, it's best to know who you are as an individual. That's the greatest experience I had exploring this topic. In times past, I would have a strong feeling about something but didn't know why. I wasn't a believer at the time, so I couldn't say it was my upbringing in Christ.

I wasn't exposed to many essentials outside of my family dynamics and culture. But I've found that our convictions are the essence of who we are. In all things, my desire is first and foremost to please God and exhibit His characteristics despite my upbringing. Having an awareness of my personal convictions has helped me establish the basis of my character. People know us through and by our convictions.

I know why my position is unmovable in certain areas. In times past, I believed I was being judgmental; sometimes I was, but oftentimes I wasn't. I didn't know how to express my convictions, especially because sometimes they appeared to be an opposition or an offense to others. I am not judging you because of my convictions. Our experiences are the basis of our convictions. Usually, a person's position, preference, or conviction regarding a matter may cause an offence to another person. That's why we stand on our convictions no matter what, because they can lead to a lonely pathway in some seasons.

Whatever you do, be committed and resilient. The things that I wouldn't move from and would stand for no matter what are the reasons I'm here today. I didn't know how to affirm myself because I didn't get much of that in my life. I was always seeking the jugular of my own life to prove to others that I could tear myself down before they could.

I was in relationships that required unrealistic expectations, however I always found myself attracted to that hurtful familiarity. It was hard to deal with in the beginning stages because it was easier to hide behind other things, and I didn't want to face the issue or grow out of it. Growing and developing comes with some tough spots and major maturity! I didn't want to keep making the same choices, but all that time, I was dealing with those choices and preferences. I knew enough to prefer something better, but I wasn't convicted and went along, being tossed to and from.

I use to fight being convicted in areas because I didn't have any idea why I felt so strongly; I didn't have any reasoning behind it. I am a logical and analytical thinker, so I would sometimes get angry when I couldn't attach reasoning to a stance or position I upheld. I would boast about being a facts kind of girl, but to my amazement, God owns the facts! The fact is conviction is progressive and powerful.

Don't feel inferior to those who have multiple convictions or have a deeper understanding of themselves and their character. We all learn over time. Conviction is a direct result of trusting the freedom to make decisions no matter what the response is. Numbers 23:19 says, "God is not a man, that he should lie; neither the son of man, that he should repent: hath he said, and shall he not do it? or hath he spoken, and shall he not make it good?" When God requests change and we accept it, He covers and backs us until that which He has spoken is fulfilled and completed.

Something happened to me in December 2017. I was working with a life coach for a push and boost to recharge my yearning to fulfill the call God has on my life. Unexpectedly, she had me do homework, and one particular assignment was challenging for me. It caused me to face a level of myself that I hadn't looked at before. I had done lessons of convictions, preferences, condemnation, forgiveness, and love, but this was something new. I was dealing with a root that was covered and buried so deep that I didn't know it was in me. When I began to receive healing in other areas of my life, this root was exposed down to its core.

There it was, looking me smack in the face: rejection. But this rejection I had was masked with a spirit of noncommittal and a strong feeling of lack of support. I do not lack confidence, but I recently had to undergo the beginning process of deliverance from this spirit of being noncommittal. That was my response to a deep, systemic root of rejection and lack of support. My response to these two areas was to stop committing to things that had the potential of hurting me or causing me to seek support from others.

At some point in my life, I convinced myself that I could do it all without any help., I would elude commitment to things and people. I completely avoided the thought of committing to things, which in turn gave the appearance that I was inconsistent. Truthfully, I did not possess the ability to commit at all. I didn't want to be on the program, but I would be at the venue, and I could help on my own terms. In other words, I always wanted to be in control of whether or not I would get hurt. I was slow to build new relationships with people because I didn't want to commit to learning about them.

I had struggled with rejection for years, so I wasn't aware that my actions were as such. I don't walk in offense or unforgiveness, so I didn't realize that rejection was leading me and causing me to shy away from my purpose and calling. It was like I had taken rejection in the form of a sword and fallen on it. I didn't receive much acceptance throughout my lifetime, so it felt familiar to be ostracized. Even today, I sometimes find myself trying to downplay who I am to fit in with others. I usually shy away from conversations that highlight great things I'm doing or are a part of. That's where the lack of support comes in. I support others, but when it sounds like I am looking for support, it gets silent.

I would receive a push from some, but the ones in my head that mattered most were usually nonexistent. There would be a faithful few supporting me, so it was very challenging to promote things I did. I strongly felt like I didn't want anyone to think I was trying to be something or was trying to do the most. I was longing to be reset. The old habits, ideologies, idioms, thoughts, and rejective thoughts that I carried had to go!

At some point, I fell victim to the confidence of the words of rejection. Rejection is a road that I will work fervently to never allow to happen again in my life. I couldn't include this as a chapter of conviction or how I am walking in freedom from it. However, I am working toward this point of conviction. I have awareness and I am being delivered, but I am not walking in full deliverance.

Releasing this book was one of the first commitments I stood on. I wrote the manuscript over four years ago, yet I struggled daily with committing to complete the process and become a published author. We all have things that are left undone, but I encourage you to get it done! Don't put off your start of change—move forward and expect to see different results! I want you to know that you are not alone in your fight!

I am not perfect, and although I truly have convictions in some areas, I am yet working in others. This is only the beginning. My desire is that you will flood my e-mail and inbox with your personal stories, testimonies, and victories. You can be a blessing to me too!

I love learning and applying what I've learned. Many of the concepts I teach come with a plan of action; it helps me understand, have an understanding, analyze, and apply what I've learned. That's my conviction, and I'm sticking to it! The below action plan is one that God has given me as I am being delivered from rejection, lack of support, and being noncommittal.

PLAN OF ACTION

- ❖ Accept the truth that you are more than a conqueror!
- ❖ Plan and keep a small commitment weekly.
- ❖ Set goals in shorter increments of time, such as monthly or quarterly versus annually.

- ❖ Get rid of unrealistic expectations!
- ❖ Pray diligently regarding people supporting you when they can.
- ❖ Set goals that are realistic and achievable within healthy timeframes.
- ❖ Let yourself off the hook. Don't speak negatively over yourself.
- ❖ Commit to your personal convictions!

Now, that wasn't too bad! I wanted to make sure I shared ways to ease into the conviction process with you. Lastly, I will say lastly there is nothing more powerful than the Word of God to stand on. Hebrews 4:12 says, "For the word of God is quick, and powerful, and sharper than any twoedged sword, piercing even to the dividing asunder of soul and spirit, and of the joints and marrow, and is a discerner of the thoughts and intents of the heart."

Discussion Questions

What does conviction mean to you?

Were you aware of the differences between convictions and preferences?

Are you confident to speak up for your beliefs in the face of death?

Do the people around you have an idea of what your convictions are?

Why do you believe God? Have you ever been challenged? What was your response, or how would you respond?

If you made a list of all your convictions, could you write down three examples or testimonies to support true conviction in those areas?

Have you experienced times when your conviction to pray was compromised? How did you recover and push through? Did you pray your way through?

Notes

Bibliography

"In Touch Ministries." The Convictions by Which We Live Series from In Touch Ministries with Charles Stanley, 2017. https://www.oneplace.com/ministries/in-touch/series/the-convictions-by-which-we-live.

Merriam-Webster.com Dictionary, s.v. "belief," accessed February 13, 2021, https://www.merriam-webster.com/dictionary/belief.

Merriam-Webster.com Dictionary, s.v. "believe," accessed February 13, 2021, https://www.merriam-webster.com/dictionary/believe.

Merriam-Webster.com Dictionary, s.v. "condemn," accessed February 13, 2021, https://www.merriam-webster.com/dictionary/condemn.

Merriam-Webster.com Dictionary, s.v. "conviction," accessed February 13, 2021, https://www.merriam-webster.com/dictionary/conviction.

Merriam-Webster.com Dictionary, s.v. "preference," accessed February 13, 2021, https://www.merriam-webster.com/dictionary/preference.

Merriam-Webster.com Dictionary, s.v. "sentence," accessed February 13, 2021, https://www.merriam-webster.com/dictionary/sentence

Shpancer, Noam. "For Sound Mental Health, Think Again About Your Thinking." Psychology Today. Sussex Publishers, September 17, 2010. https://www.psychologytoday.com/us/blog/insight-therapy/201009/sound-mental-health-think-again-about-your-thinking.

Youngblood, Ronald F., ed. "Conviction." In *Nelson's New Illustrated Bible Dictionary: an Authoritative One-Volume Reference Work on the Bible*, 296–96. Nashville, TN: Thomas Nelson, Inc, 1995.

Printed in the United States
By Bookmasters